# Meet the LLLamas

## From The Small Friends Research Institute
## And Tall Cat Productions
©Susan Gainen, Artist & Chief Whimsy Officer

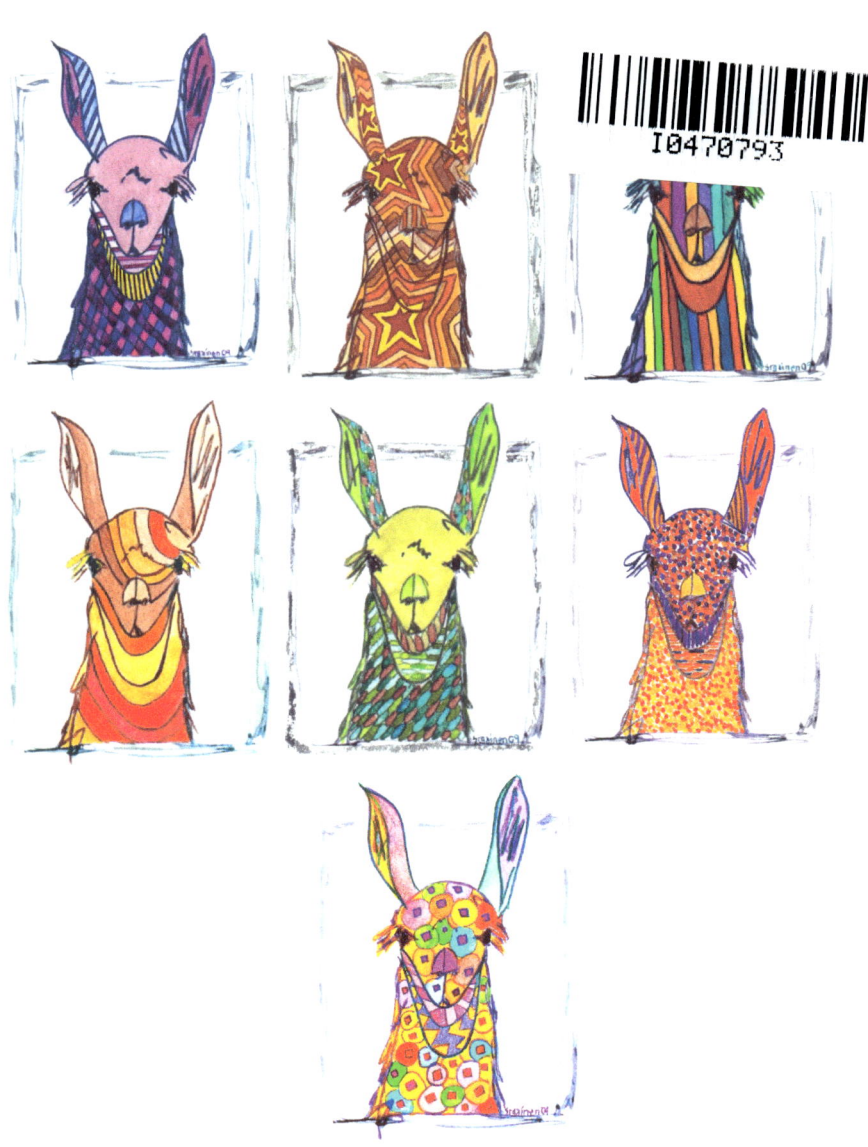

## Susan Gainen paints in four ways:

Geometric abstractions: original watercolors called *nanoscapes*
*Small Friends*: whimsical creatures' original watercolor portraits
*Other visions*: tiny original watercolors & Photoshop™ make magic
*"Lost Cave Paintings of Saint Paul"* from an unexcavated cave

## Find more of Susan Gainen's art and writing at:

**The Small Friends' website & blog**
http://www.susangainen-nanoscapes-smallfriends.com/
*The Small Friends' Chronicles* (softcover & ebook)
70-pages of whimsical creatures' portraits and stories
http://www.blurb.com/bookstore/detail/3479674

**The nanoscapes' website & blog**
http://www.susangainen-nanoscapes.com/

**Small Friends & nanoscapes' images on cool products**
http://www.zazzle.com/susangainen

**Small Friends & nanoscapes images on Fabric & Wallpaper**
http://www.spoonflower.com/profiles/susangainen

**Contact: susangainen@comcast.net**

### Thanks to
### The Small Friends Research Institute
### Tall Cat Productions

Table of Contents

# Introduction

Since 2009, when Susan Gainen found that she had dozens of leftover LLLama portraits, she planned to create a genealogy to sort out their relationships. It was an important project, but it remained stuck on her "to-do" list until 2012.

## LLLamas to the rescue

She began her first Image-a-Day painting project on Facebook in October 2009 with pumpkins, and continued month-by-month with leaves, Hanukah candles & snowflakes, left handed gloves, missing socks, basketballs, and raindrops. When she ran out of ideas for May, the LLLamas stepped up and were introduced on Facebook. They then joined her abstracts on the nanoscapes website.

## LLLamas end confusion

By early 2010, the presence of the LLLamas and other whimsical creatures on the nanoscapes website was confusing to everyone. They needed to separate, and in June 2010, Rainbow LLLama and 30 other small friends left the nanoscapes and launched the small friends' website and blog. The remaining LLLamas went on a WorLLLd Tour from which they have just returned.

The LLLama Families donated their archives and portrait collection to the Small Friends Research Institute, giving life to projects just like this one.

## Tall Cat

Spokescat, Small Friends
October 2012

# Rainbow LLLama
## The Official SpokesLLLama
## For all of the LLLama Families

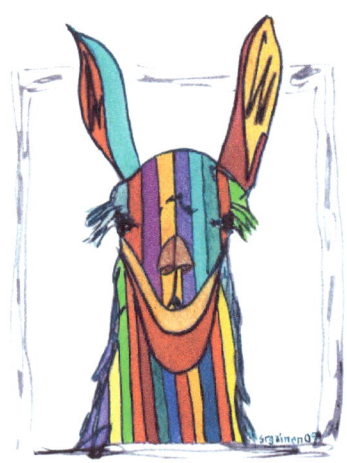

## "WeLLLcome to our worLLLd."

**Rainbow LLLama** is a public relations specialist who has advised sticky-fingered politicians, troubled CEOs, and actors with behavior issues. He measures his success by knowing that on his watch, their public reputations remained intact.

As SpokesLLLama, he is a great favorite of journalists and bloggers because he respects the 24/7 nature of news and the primacy of facts. He also courteously spells out the hard words and speaks slowly and clearly so that he can be heard on TV, radio, and YouTube.

He has many friends of all stripes, colors, species, shapes, and perspectives. He wishes that all of the attention that is being devoted to denying rights to his GLBT LLLama friends would be focused on important things such as bringing world peace, curing cancer, and solving world hunger.

# The Original Technolama:
## Greetings and a word about spellling

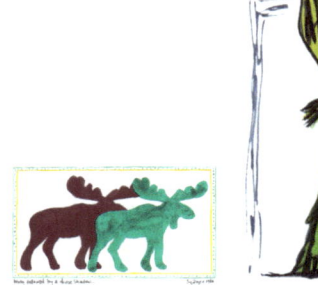 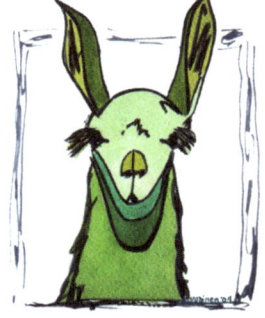 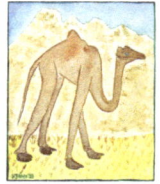

Matt and Jess had admired the Small Friends' dromedary (*One hump or two?*) and Moose (*Being Followed by a Moose Shadow*), and in 2009 they asked whether Susan would create a logo for Matt's new company "Technolama."

She suggested "… a llama's head coming out of a laptop" and they agreed. They selected one among the 20 unique llama drawings, and, then one among 24 painted LLLamas. Knowing he would look good as a tiny logo, this one became The Technolama.

From the one (**The Original Technolama**) came a flock of LLLamas, each with a story, a world view, or a fashion statement.

# We choose the speLLLing.
# These are our stories.

# Purple LLLamas

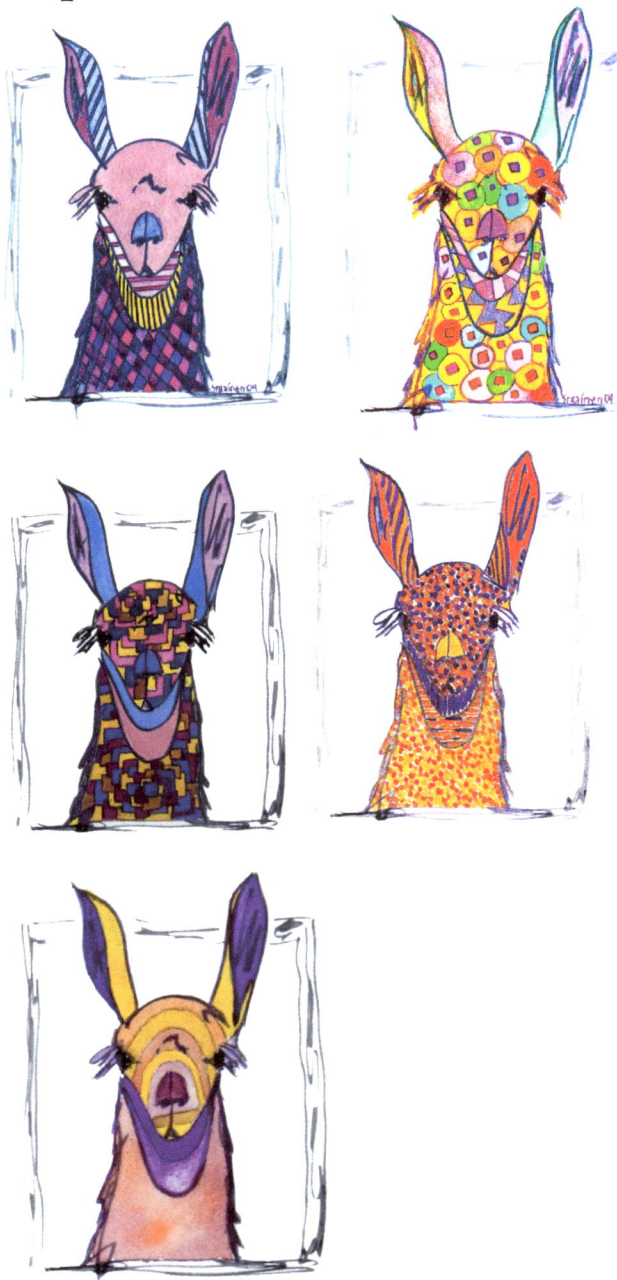

# Ernest Purple LLLama

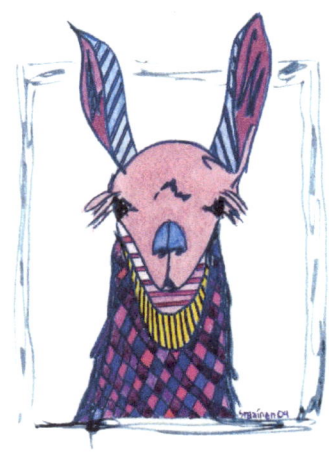

**Ernest Purple LLLama** is a college professor who teaches two courses in LLLama AnthropoLLLogy. His dissertation, ***"Forget the Vikings: the LLLamas were here first,"*** has sold just 137 hardback copies, but its ebook is climbing steadily in the Amazon rankings.

Ernest PLL (to his friends) and "Professor Purple" to his students, is a beloved teacher who combines a keen wit and an encyclopedic knowledge of his subject, and the rare enthusiasm for making it accessible and exciting to students.

He is known for his contributions to useful and practical academic collaborations with international political and cultural historians, bioarchaeologists, and cultural anthropologists.

# Candy Wafer LLLama

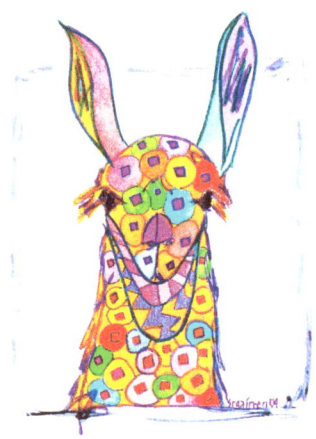

**Candy Wafer LLLama** was SpokesLLLama for several international candy companies until they were merged out of independent existence. She was "replaced," if you can call it that, by a giggling animated candy bar.

Since leaving the candy business, Candy Wafer has taken the lead among her peers with an international non-denominational non-profit that cares for retired Easter Bunnies. She blogs in support of the growing **Peeps®** families, and is a lobbyist for **Safety First: Keep Peeps® Out of Microwaves.**

Although she has no direct connection to the makers of **NECCO®** wafers and candy hearts, her heart belongs to them.

# Purple Tattoo LLLama

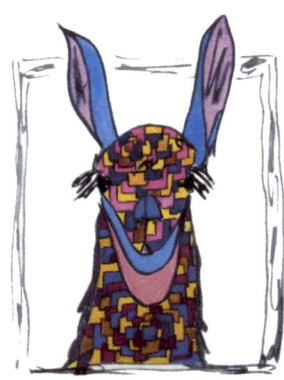

Every family has a rebel, and **Purple Tattoo LLLama** is the LLLeader of the Pack for his generation.

Even as a baby lllama (cria), Purple Timmy (his real name) was full of mischief. He led his siblings and cousins on adventures into the woods and across streams. Inevitably, they came home after curfew covered with mud and twigs. He remains unrepentent.

He was a gifted student. His exam grades always blew out the curve, and he was an annoying smartie-pants in class. Nonetheless, his parents fretted during his extra-sullen teen years. Little did they know that he was working hard at emulating his movie idol, James Dean.

Teenage Purple Timmy patiently saved his paper route money for the full-body tattoos which he designed himself. When they were complete, he changed his name to Purple Tattoo and set off for Hollywood where he has worked steadily in memorably sullen character parts. He is a LLLama of few words but plenty of attitude.

# Purple Camo LLLama

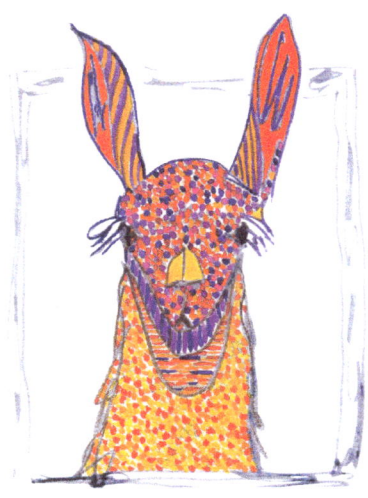

You might be surprised at the opportunities in undercover work for LLLamas and other Small Friends. Many work in elite organizations preventing cyber attacks, uncovering other kinds of industrial espionage, and exposing evil doers around the world. **Purple Camo LLLama** and **Small Friend Zavier Camo Zebra** have an extraordinarily lucrative partnership. Watch out Skulduggers and Miscreants!

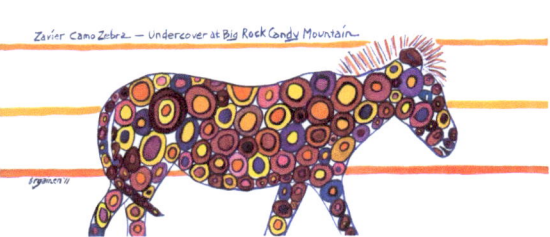

Zavier Camo Zebra, undercover at the Big Rock Candy Mountain. He is featured in **"The Small Friends' Chronicles."**

# Quiet Purple LLLama

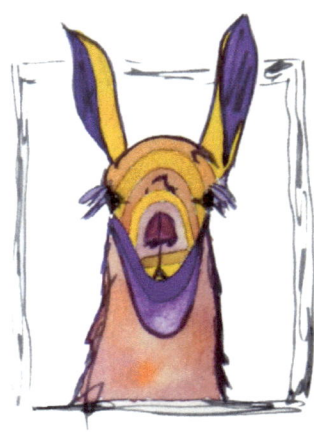

**Quiet Purple** is the most private of all LLLamas.

Although part of the most exuberant LLLama family, she stays in the shadows. She considered changing her name to "no-name," but didn't want to make extra work for the LLLama Registry staff.

Although rumors abound about her career as spy master, currency manipulator or oil speculator, she fiercely protects her privacy. Some of the youngest LLLamas watch for clues to these mysteries and regularly compare notes to see if she has inadvertently revealed any secrets.

She has had no electronic presence other than a brief appearance on the small friends' website (which she immediately ordered taken down). She is not on Facebook or LinkedIn, and her smart phone is set to "dumb."

# Green LLLamas

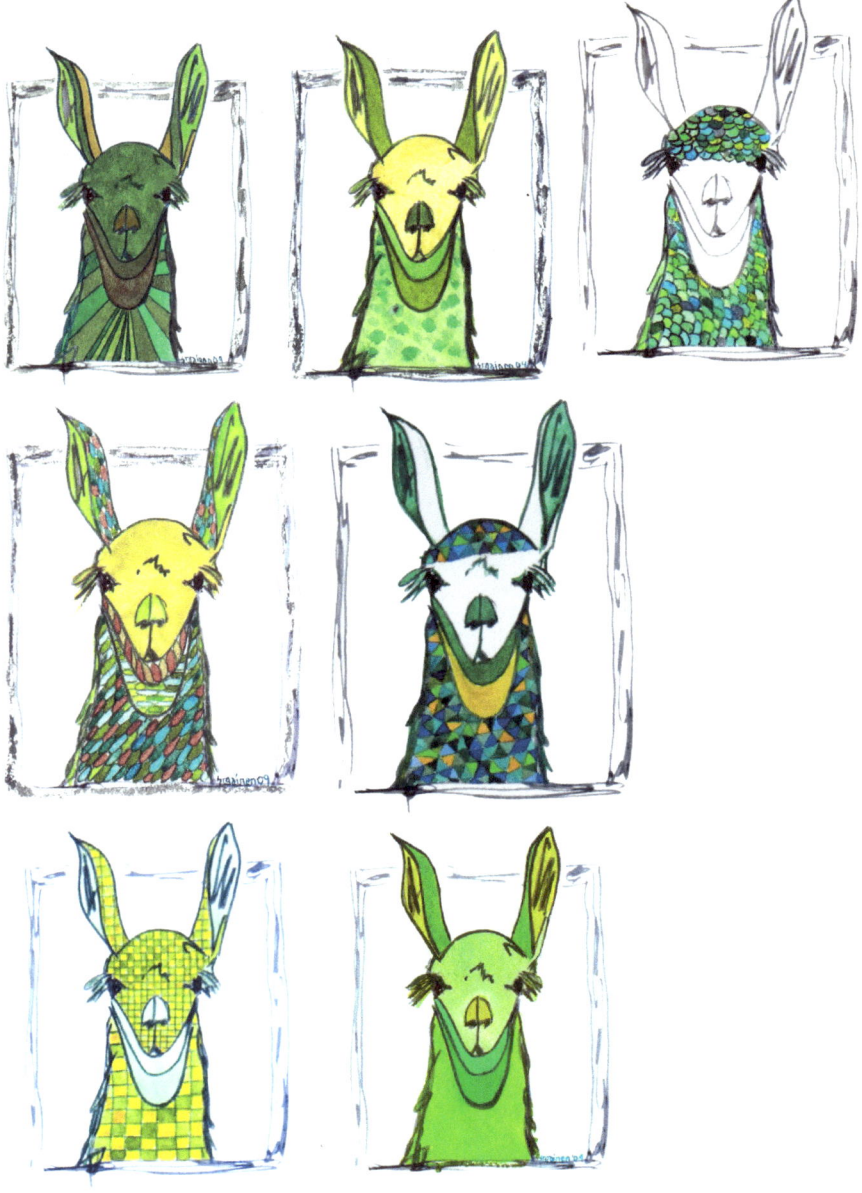

# Forest Green Patriarch LLLama

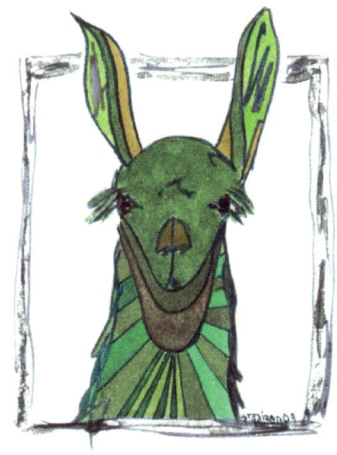

**Forest Green Patriarch LLLama** heads the Green LLLama family, the oldest LLLama family.

He is famously particular about ceremony and protocol, especially when addressing problems presented by the Lesser Green LLLamas. Anyone who asks for favors must perform The LLLama Dance which includes some very deep knee bends that are the equivalent of the St. James Bow done by debutants when presented at Debutante Balls. There is some concern about long-term knee damage and arthritis brought on by frequent participation in this ceremony, but the LLLamas have excellent health insurance.

Patriarch's concern for rules and protocol has led him to establish a LLLamas-only chapter of the American Institute of Parliamentarians. His avocation is promoting the effective use of democratic parliamentary principles, and he is working on an adaptation of Robert's Rules of Order for Official LLLama Family Meetings.

# Green Tie-Dye LLLama

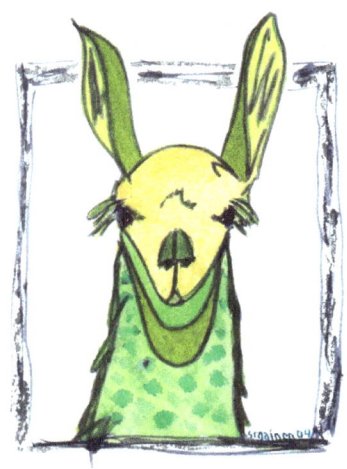

**Green Tie-Dye LLLama** was influential behind the scenes with many 60s rock groups' costume design teams, and he was one of the first to connect psychedelic light shows, theater lighting, and fabric design.

He remains a stickler for the use of authentic batik tools and techniques, and for hand-crafted tie-dye. Coming out of retirement in 2012, he is creating a collection for launch at Bryant Park which will incorporate references to the sixties (batik and tie-dye) and the seventies (platform shoes, wide-legged jeans, and jersey dresses).

As he is true to his commitment to authenticity, he is not concerned about coordinating his vision with 21st century fashionistas.

# Loretta, Italian LLLama Grand-Mama

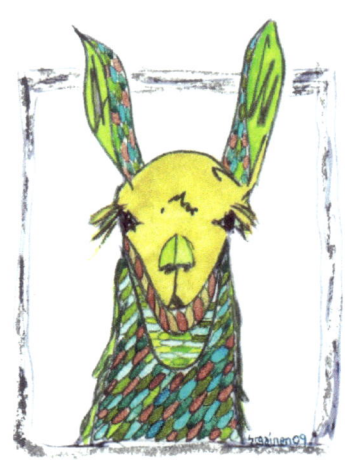

**Loretta, Italian LLLama Grand-Mama,** is very proud that her fur reminds people of the individual grains of rice in a proper risotto. She recognizes that the colors of her fur might not resemble everyone's favorite flavors, but she is deeply fond of mushroom and basil risotto and serves it every Sunday night to a growing crowd of children, grandchildren and friends.

The Italian LLLama families lived for centuries in the foothills of Mont Blanc in Italy. Shortly after work began on the Mont Blanc Tunnel in 1957, they moved to a secluded location in upstate New York. They are now close enough to reach excellent Italian markets, but far enough away from the City to lead contemplative lives.

Loretta's granddaughter, Lola LLLama, is writing a cookbook called "My Grand-Mama's Risotto Rocks."

# Undersea LLLama

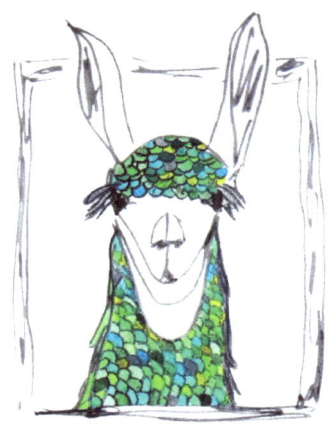

Once she learned that oceans cover 70 percent of the earth's surface, **Undersea LLLama** began to pay attention to the apparently unchecked dumping that has led to the appearance of large floating islands of plastic waste, and to the acidification of ocean water. She now travels throughout the world, tirelessly campaigning to protect the sea.

She is appalled and frightened for the future of humans (of course) and her aquatic Small Friends including Ancient Nile Bulti-Fish, Sally Seahorse, Nedi Needlepoint Fish, Olivia Orange Fish, Raul Red Fish, Harry Herringbone Fish, and Sally Striped Bass, who are all featured in "The Small Friends' Chronicles."

Having been told often that her fur makes her look like a mermaid, she also has growing concern for her heretofore undiscovered mermaid cousins. At her behest, The Small Friends' Research Institute launched a "Mermaid Protection Project" in 2011.

# Stained Glass LLLama

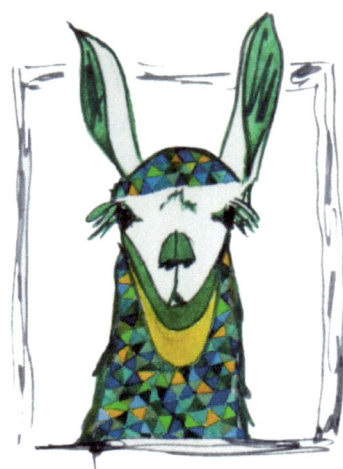

**Stained Glass LLLama** is a disciple of Tiffany and a collector of windows and other glass dating back to the Renaissance.

He is also a committed collector of examples of four centuries of glass from LLLithuania. His own master glass piece, "GLLLas LLLamas: Our world view," should be completed by 2016. Sight unseen, it has been acquired for a whopping price by a Very Smart Collector.

Stained Glass LLLama is sixth cousin to the famous Small Friends Hernando Stained Glass Hippo and to Tiny Stained Glass Hippo from 7 Hippos Marching.

Small Friends Institute geneticists and art historians are trying to determine the relationships between and among the other Stained Glass animals, including Sarah Stained Glass Cat, Amelia Tall Glazed Window Cat, and Rav Stained Glass Running Elephant.

# Green Gingham LLLama

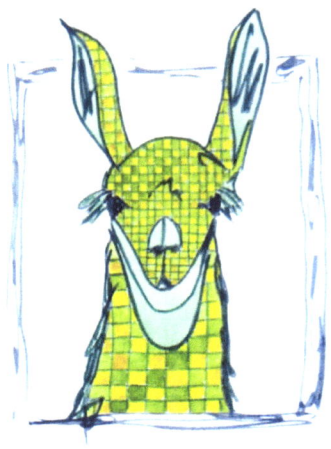

**Green Gingham LLLama** loves color and fabric. He co-owns a fabric and yarn store with **Small Friend Bird Brain** (featured in "The Small Friends' Chronicles"), and they are always experimenting with new tools and techniques. They are looking for someone to teach quilting and fabric embellishment.

Together, they teach sewing, knitting, and needlepoint classes, encouraging both young and chronologically-enriched customers to experiment, to make mistakes (from which they will learn a lot), and to celebrate creativity.

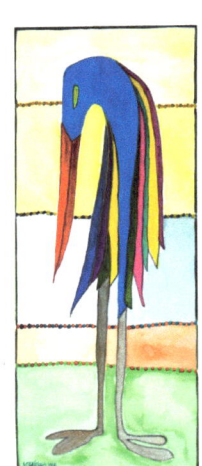

When their customers earn prizes at the Minnesota State Fair, Gingham and Bird Brain invite them to display their works and ribbons at the store.

**Bird Brain**

# Quiet Green LLLama

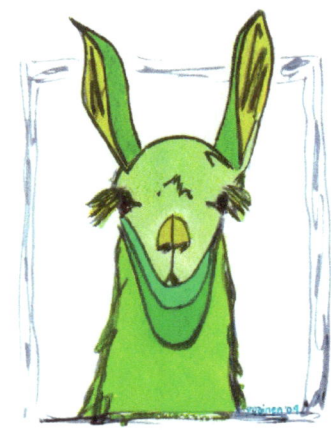

**Quiet Green LLLama** is The Technolama's twin. They look enough alike as to have been the subject of a study to determine whether they are identical or fraternal. (They are fraternal.)

While the Technolama has had great adventures as front-llama for Matt's tech company, **Quiet Green** has been supremely happy as a school teacher. For the past 20 years, he has taught Composition and Grammar, LLLama LLLiterature: Literary LLLamas in the 19th and 20th Centuries, and The Poetical LLLamas and their Influence on the Victorian Poets.

Fighting against a tidal wave of nonsensical pedagogy, Quiet Green has always taught each of the parts of speech, grammar, composition, and sentence diagramming. Sticking very closely to the lessons from Warriner's *English Grammar and Composition* (Harcourt Brace, 1957) he makes certain that each of his students can construct simple and complex sentences, tightly woven paragraphs, and essays.

He is a strong supporter of The Hochman Program created by Judith Hochman of Windward School. When interviewed in *The Atlantic* (The Writing Revolution, Peg Tyre, October 2012), Hochman said "…kids need a formula, at least a first, because what we are asking them to do is very difficult. So let's stop acting like they should just know how to do it. Give them a formula! Later, when they understand the rules of good writing, they can figure out how to break them."

# Blue LLLamas

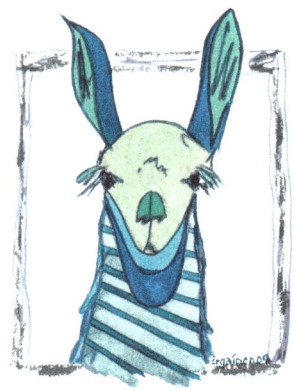

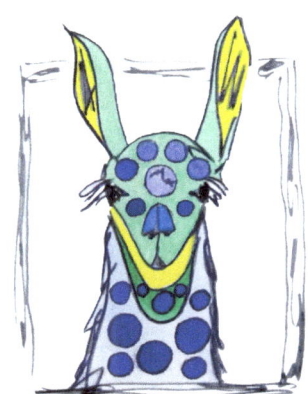

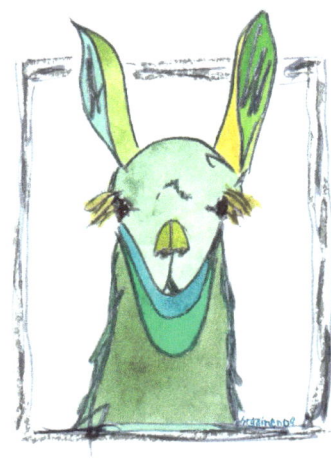

# Blu-een LLLama

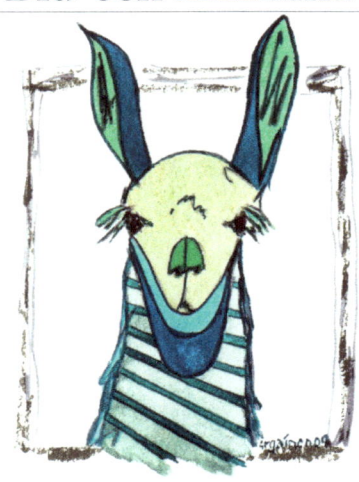

**Blu-een LLLama** believes that he is the luckiest of LLLamas because his birth brought peace between two families that had been at odds for generations. The Blue and Green LLLama family feuds' origins had been lost in the mists of time. Because it involved audacious pranks but no serious personal injury, it vaguely reminded observers of a mild version of the legendary Hatfield and McCoy dust-up.

When His BLLLue LLLama Mama married his Green LLLama Dad, the goodwill from the week-long celebration allowed old arguments and bad feelings to dissipate and then to disappear. Could humans learn from the LLLamas? Perhaps they should use this allrecipes.com **Party Punch** recipe.

**Combine in a pitcher:** 1 cup fresh lime juice, 2 cups simple syrup, 3 cups amber rum, 4 c orange juice, 4 dashes bitters, fresh grated nutmeg

**Pour over ice.** Consider making a Ginger or Ginger/Chili Simple Syrup.

# Blue Dot LLLama

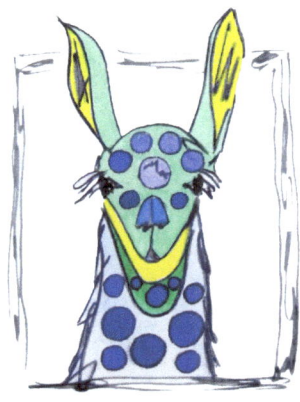

Since childhood, **Blue Dot LLLama's** favorite foods have been blue potatoes and blueberries.

Somewhat exasperated, his mother often said, "If you keep eating blue potatoes and blueberries, you will turn blue." Not surprisingly, she was correct.

Happily for Blue Dot, he is a natural connoisseur of The Blues, and he owns a very hip bar and restaurant called "My Blues Heaven & Potato Palace."

On the menu:

Blue corn and blue cheese quesadillas
Blueberry & blue corn pancakes
Blueberry Pie
Blueberry Crisp
Cooked Poppy Seed Milkshakes
Blue Mashed Potato Bar
Blueberry Chili Chutney

Blueberry & blue corn muffins
Blue Potato Sheppard's Pie
Blueberry Buckle
Blue Crab Cakes
Blue Curacao-based drinks
Blueberry Wine

# Blue Green LLLama

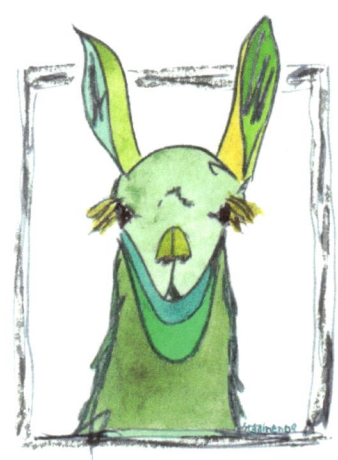

The **Blue Green LLLama** works quietly in the shadows with Veterinarians Without Borders, taking startling and life-threatening risks to rescue LLLamas and other creatures who are caught in natural disasters and human conflagrations.

He is a first cousin of the Technolama, and proud of his cousin's success. They grew up together, frolicking as young LLLamas do. Their practical jokes were infamous, but always in good spirits. Their favorite foods were Chocolate Cupcakes which they ate by the dozens, Cheese Curds (imported from Wisconsin, of course), and calzone stuffed with pepperoni.

One of Blue Green's colleagues in Veterinarians Without Borders acted courageously to save Peter Pangolin, a Small Friend who now thrives as a truffle hunter in France. Peter is a great friend of The French LLLama.

# Red LLLamas

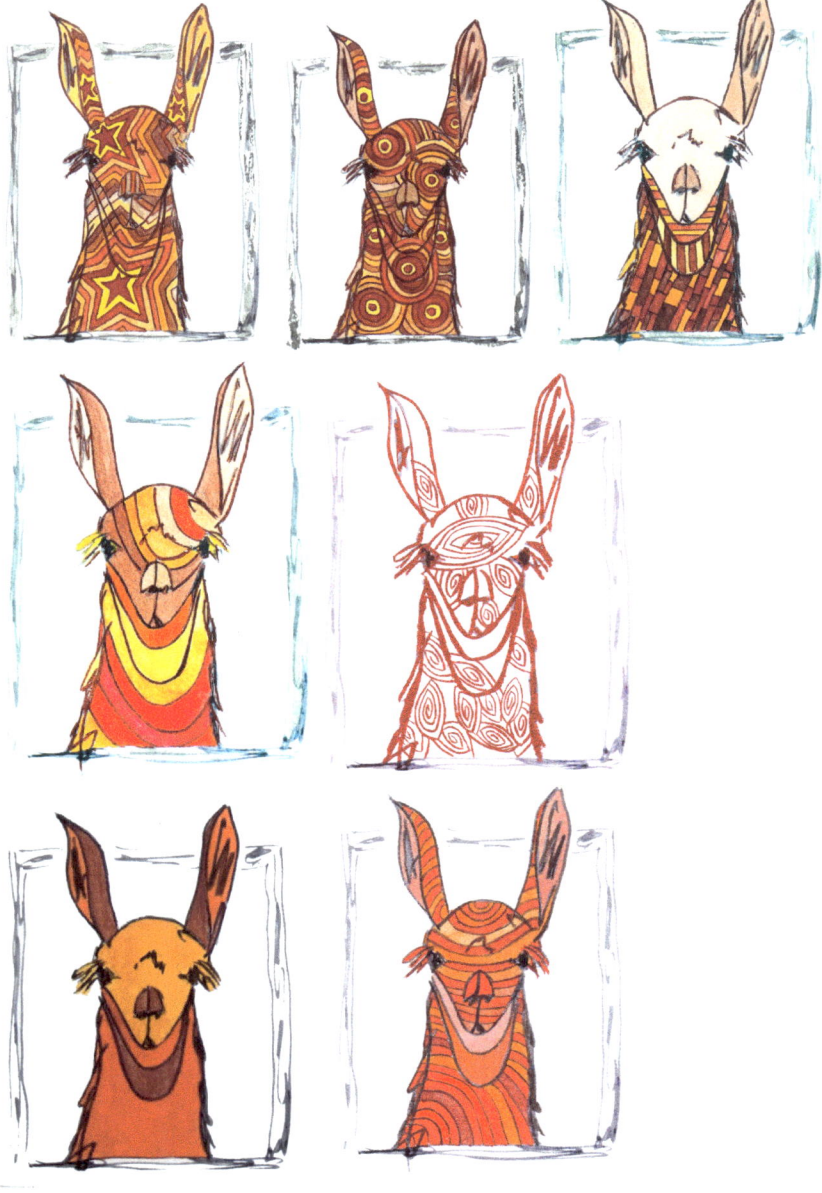

# Target LLLama

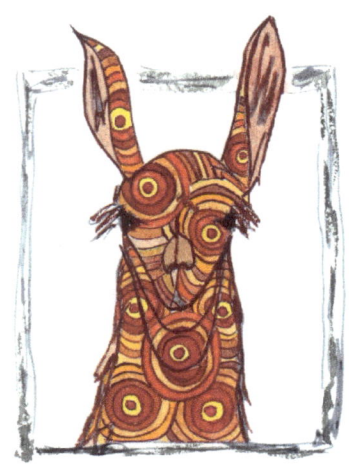

**Target LLLama** is part of the Art and Red LLLama Families. She celebrates concentric circles, which have appeared in art, architecture, contour farming, mazes, and crop circles for thousands of years. She is interested – no, really, she is obsessed – with alien incursions, Saturn's rings, and lunar eclipses. She is a great supporter of artists who work at the intersection of geometric abstraction, science fiction and fantasy, and very modern expressionistic dance.

Much loved by her siblings and cousins, they are fiercely protective of her privacy, her passions, and her various therapies. Target often wears a LLLama BaseBaLLL cap lined with aluminum foil to protect her from "The Rays." She has strong opinions about pink helicopters, too.

# Star, the Original Diva LLLama

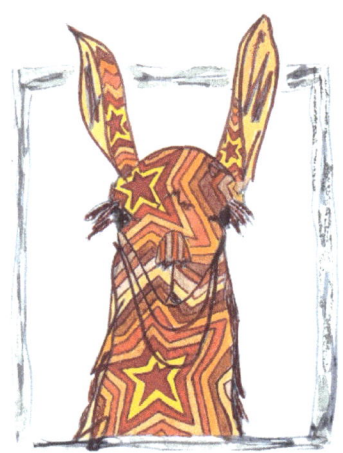

**Star, the Original Diva LLLama,** has been front-row center in every photo since she was two years old. She has starred in many theatrical productions including all of her elementary school talent shows, every play or musical in junior high, high school, and college, and more than 100 regional and off-off Broadway productions.

The only glitch in her career was a brief and very unhappy project in which she starred (of course) as a mime. She spent a great deal of money to secure and destroy all of the copies of "Mime LLLama, Myself."

At great risk to her highly-insured self, she does her own stunts. Generous to a fault, she signs autographs for free, and is a major donor to LLLamas Without Borders.

# French LLLama

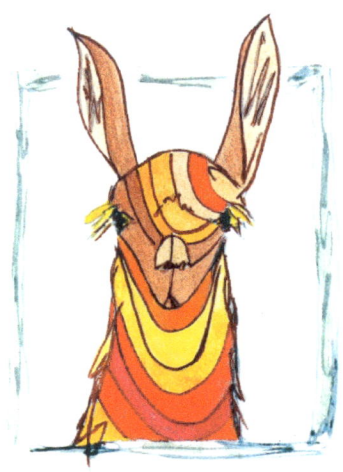

**French LLLama** wears a beret as a badge of his French Honor. He has welcomed his Small Friend Peter Pangolin to France, and takes great delight in accompanying him on his monthly trips to Paris. They stroll along the Champs-Elysées, eat Peter's favorite food (chocolate truffles), and visit Sacha Finkelsztajn's Boulangerie on Rue des Rosiers for the best apple cake in the world.

Like so many French folk, he is deeply saddened by the arrival of American Fast Food into France.

Learn more about Peter Pangolin and other small friends in "The Small Friends' Chronicles," a 70-page collection of whimsical creatures' portraits and stories (softcover and ebook).

# Red-Headed Stranger LLLama

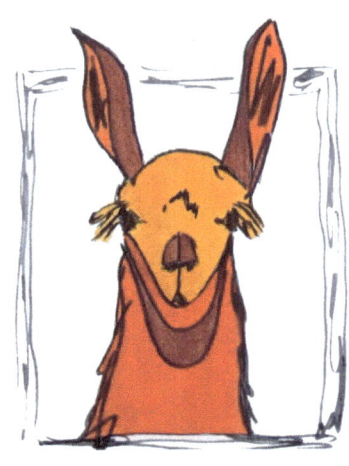

**Red-Headed Stranger LLLama** works for a very secret organization which cannot be named. His skillset will give you a clue about his activities, though. He speaks seven languages, programs the most complex computer systems in the world, has BLLLack Belts in four martial arts, and can pour any drink anyone might ever ask for.

# Satellite LLLama

**Satellite LLLama** honors the service and sacrifice of the men, women, and LLLamas who have ventured into space.

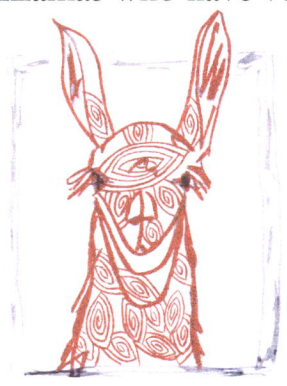

# Brick LLLama

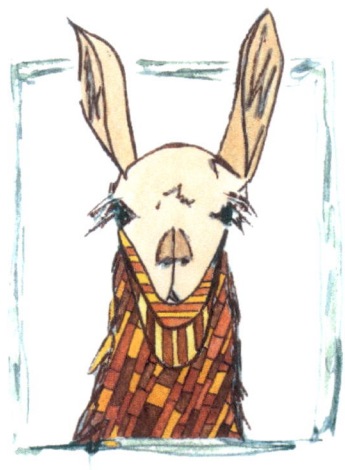

**Brick LLLama** is an architect because his Mother read an important book to him.

When Brick was a young child (a cria), his mother read Karl Sabbagh's **Skyscraper: The Making of a Building**. They also watched the five-part PBS series that was based on the book, which tells the story of Manhattan's One Worldwide Plaza from conception to construction. Brick has seen the video 76 times.

His favorite part of the book explains how the large pieces of steel are fabricated, transported to New Jersey where they are stored on a big field, and then driven "just in time" to the worksite as needed. He was fascinated by the science and the structures, the logistics of design and construction, the relationships between and among bankers, tenants, architects, contractors, subcontractors, vendors, and construction workers.

Brick specializes in designing multi-family LLLama communities, and all of his projects are state-of-the-art in recycled materials, construction techniques, and energy management.

# Red Velvet LLLama

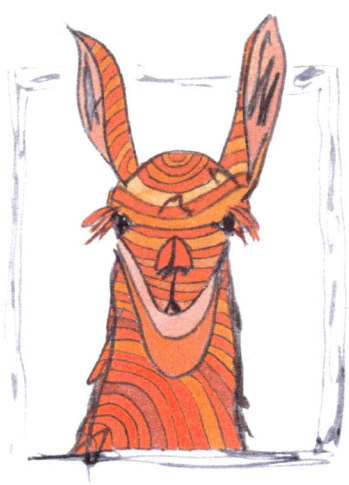

Blythly ignoring the fact that Red Velvet Cake first appeared on menus in the 1920s, **Red Velvet LLLama** holds tight to her belief that the cake is named after her.

It has always been her birthday and random celebration cake, and she brings it to pot luck suppers on a special footed cake plate so that it can't be missed.

Of course, red is her favorite color, and she uses it with abandon in every room in her house. She also wanted to paint her house bright red, but her plan was opposed by her neighbors, who complained to the community association. Expensive litigation ensued, and Red lost.

Revenge is sweet, and Red won in the end. She planted her entire yard with trees and shrubs with red leaves or red fruit. All of her perennial and annual plantings have red leaves or red flowers. She grows 14 varieties of tomatoes and seven varieties of peppers, which she doesn't pick until they are bright red. One of her favorite plants is Pineapple Sage. Although its leaves are green, it has a stunning red flower in the fall.

# Beach LLLamas

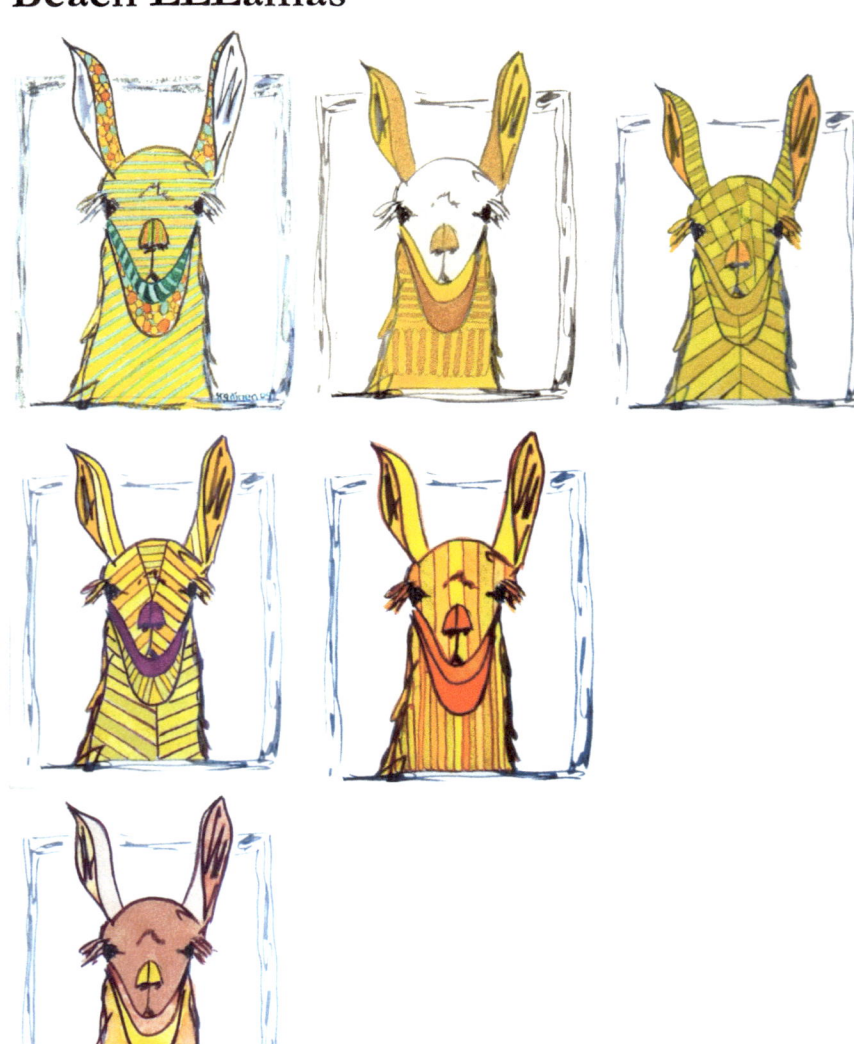

# Awning LLLama

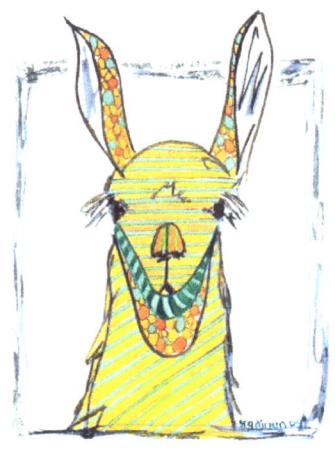

**Awning LLLama** is head of the Beach LLLama Family.

It is not widely known, but LLLamas can be found all over the world: on mountaintops, in deserts, in large cities, and in small towns.

Awning and his friends sometimes live on cunningly decorated houseboats and occasionally in tiny beach cottages with awnings that provide protective coloration to keep the paparazzi at bay.

With top-tier international art gallery representation, Beach LLLamas Families' sea-glass and starfish sculptures are part of many public and private art collections. Although he is generally reclusive, Awning conducts an annual sea-glass creativity workshop. Its seats sell out in minutes.

He always leaves the beach during Spring Break.

# Cousins from the Southwest

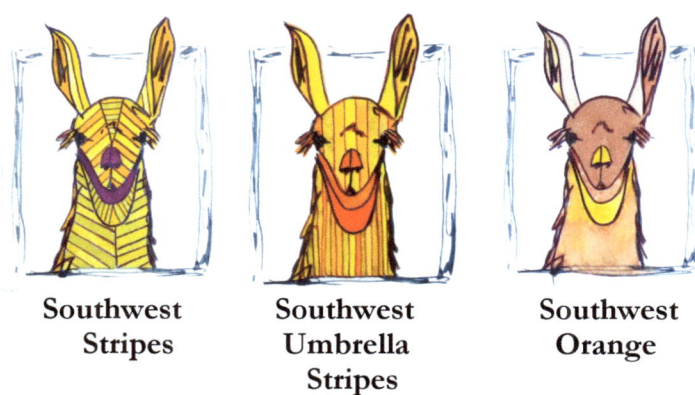

**Southwest Stripes**  **Southwest Umbrella Stripes**  **Southwest Orange**

The presence of camels in the American Southwest is a little-known but well-established story. They were introduced by the US Army in 1856. Their legendary ability to go without water served everyone well on survey missions in what became Colorado until the outbreak of the Civil War, when the "Camel Project" was abandoned.

Less well known is the presence of LLLamas in the Desert Southwest. A small group moved to California shortly after the Gold Rush began. In early 1859, however, when it was clear that the bulk of the gold would be found in the chillier parts of Northern California and in Alaska, they promptly departed for warmer climates.

The **Southwest LLLamas** are descended from the Beach and Orange LLLama families. They are resourceful and smart, and they cultivate a particularly hot orange chili pepper. The cousins' prize pepper is called Orange Blast. It ranks at 150,000 Scoville units.

# Executive Director LLLama

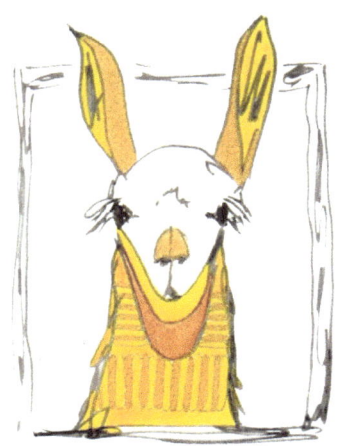

**Executive Director LLLama** has all of the hyper-efficient, quiet dignity, and iron-fist-in-velvet-glove characteristics that anyone would want in someone who manages the world-wide philanthropic umbrella organization that includes LLLamas Without Borders, Multi-LLLingual LLLama LLLibraries, International Gallery of the LLLama, and Feed the LLLamas. Don't mess with her.

Even as a child, ED excelled at organization. In junior high and high school, she started Youth LLLeague Volleyball, the LLLama Drama Society, and LLLeaping LLLamas, a track-and-field competition.

As a completely organized LLLama, she has always been able to balance work and family.

# Chief Farmer LLLama

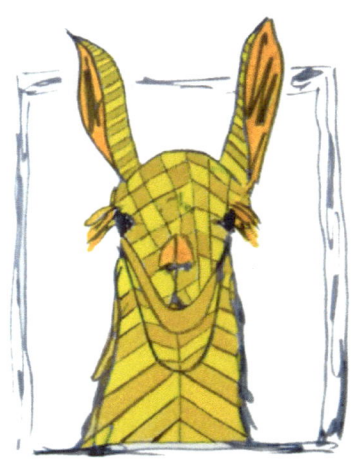

Each year **Chief Farmer LLLama** works hard to have both straight and contour rows to ensure the best yield using the hill, rivers, and streams on his property. He and other Farmer LLLamas are extremely talented developers and managers of micro-climates, growing sugarcane (for LLLoLLLipops, a LLLama favorite), vaniLLLa beans, chiLLLi peppers, diLLL, and garLLLic. They are also major importers of aLLLspice.

*The Complete Guide to LLLama Farms and Gardens*, a work in progress, has an expected publication date of 2014.

Chief Farmer LLLama and his friends blog at
www.farmerlllama.blllogllog.com

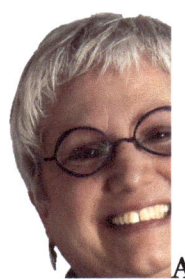

## ABOUT THE AUTHOR

Susan Gainen is a painter, writer, national speaker, and occasional cooking teacher.

She celebrates chronological enrichment, universal whimsy, and the magic of detail. She paints in four ways:

1. The **nanoscapes** are original watercolor geometric abstractions. They started as tiny paintings and grew larger when a friend said "I love your work, but I can't put a postcard behind my sofa."

2. The **Small Friends** are the whimsical creatures who have visited or moved into her studio to share stories and to pose for their portraits.

3. The **other visions** are a collection of 2012 Image-a-day paintings made when original tiny watercolors meet Photoshop™ and turn into digital magic.

4. The premise of **The Lost Cave Paintings of Saint Paul** is that among the caves in Saint Paul which were famously used by bootleggers during Prohibition, that there is probably an undiscovered cave whose walls are covered with paintings of historic, prehistoric, and whimsical creatures.

When not painting or entertaining Small Friends and human friends, she travels the country to speak about career-related issues with Pass the Baton llc (her consulting business), teaches occasional cooking classes with susan-cooks! (her modest cooking school), and reads mysteries. She is supervised by two cats, Phil and Max, whose motto is "If it moves it's mine; if I can make it move, it's mine."